Presented to

Peggy S. Noyes

On the occasion of

_____

From

_____

Date

_____

WHAT WOULD JESUS DO?

BARBOUR
PUBLISHING, INC.

What Would Jesus Do?

What would you do in a certain situation? What would Jesus do? The answer might not always be the same. It always comes down to WWJD. Jesus will never steer you wrong.

With its emphasis on developing a Christlike mind-set, WWJD is the latest craze for Christian teenagers. But did you know that it all started when your great-great-grandparents were your age?

WWJD is the focus of Charles M. Sheldon's classic 1896 novel *In His Steps,* about a pastor who shakes up his congregation, and his entire community, by pledging to ask "What would Jesus do?" before making any decisions, however large or small. It was a good idea a century ago, and it's still a good idea today.

You're already familiar with WWJD. Now, get to know *In His Steps.* This book includes passages from the book, corresponding verses from the Bible, prayers, and quotes—all will help you determine "What would Jesus do?"

So now, what will you do?

WHAT WOULD JESUS DO?

If any man will come after me, let him deny himself, and take up his cross daily, and follow me. Luke 9:23

· · · · · ·

"What do you mean when you sing 'I'll go with Him, with Him, all the way?' Do you mean that you are suffering and denying yourselves and trying to save lost, suffering humanity just as I understand Jesus did?"

from In His Steps

· · · · · ·

" 'Love thy neighbor' is a precept which could transform the world if it were universally practiced."

—Mary McLeod Bethune

This is my commandment, That ye love one another, as I have loved you. John 15:12

. . . . . .

"It seems to me there's an awful lot of trouble in the world that somehow wouldn't exist if all the people who sing such songs went and lived them out."

from *In His Steps*

. . . . . .

Father, help me to live out Your love.

Dear Jesus, help me pick up my cross today and follow You.

Greater love hath no man than this, that a man lay down his life for his friends. Ye are my friends, if ye do whatsoever I command you.
John 15:13–14

• • • • • •

"You have been good to me. Somehow I feel as if it was what Jesus would do."

from *In His Steps*

• • • • • •

"Love doesn't just sit there like a stone, it has to be made, like bread."

—Ursula K. LeGuin

For even hereunto were ye called: because Christ also suffered for us, leaving us an example, that ye should follow his steps.
1 Peter 2:21

. . . . . .

"I want volunteers from the First Church who will pledge themselves, earnestly and honestly for an entire year, not to do anything without first asking the question, 'What would Jesus do?' And after asking that question, each one will follow Jesus as exactly as he knows how, no matter what the result may be."

from *In His Steps*

"We cannot separate His demands from His love. We cannot dissect Jesus and relate only to the parts that we like."

—Rebecca Manley Pippert

• • • • • •

"Give all you have, as well as all you are, a spiritual sacrifice to him who withheld not from you his Son, his only Son. . . ."

—John Wesley

• • • • • •

Help me, Jesus, to give everything to You: my money, my possessions, my talents, my time, my love.

Be ye therefore followers of God, as dear children; And walk in love, as Christ also hath loved us, and hath given himself for us an offering and a sacrifice to God.
Ephesians 5:1–2

· · · · · ·

"Our motto will be, 'What would Jesus do?' Our aim will be to act just as He would if He was in our places, regardless of immediate results."

from *In His Steps*

· · · · · ·

Dear Lord, let me act today the way You would if You were in my place. I want to be God's follower, His dear child.

If any of you lack wisdom, let him ask of God, that giveth to all men liberally, and upbraideth not; and it shall be given him. James 1:5

. . . . . .

"I am a little in doubt as to the source of our knowledge concerning what Jesus would do. Who is to decide for me just what He would do in my case? It is a different age. There are many perplexing questions in our civilization that are not mentioned in the teachings of Jesus. How am I going to tell what He would do?"

from *In His Steps*

. . . . . .

"Don't worry about what you do not understand.... Worry about what you do understand [in the Bible] but do not live by."

—Corrie ten Boom

13

· ·

Help me, dear Lord,
to hear the Spirit's voice
speaking in my life.

· ·

Then spake Jesus again unto them, saying, I am the light of the world: he that followeth me shall not walk in darkness, but shall have the light of life. John 8:12

. . . . . .

"But when it comes to a genuine, honest, enlightened following of Jesus' steps, I cannot believe there will be any confusion either in our own minds or in the judgment of others."

from *In His Steps*

. . . . . .

I don't want to walk in the dark, Lord Jesus.
I want Your Spirit's light to fill my life.

Master, I will follow thee whithersoever thou goest. Matthew 8:19

. . . . . .

"After we have asked the Spirit to tell us what Jesus would do and have received an answer to it, we are to act regardless of the results to ourselves."

from *In His Steps*

. . . . . .

"Let nothing deter you. . .remember it is God who has called you and it is the same as when He called Moses or Samuel."

—Gladys Aylward

. . . .

In each thing that happens
today, Lord, show me what
You would do.

. . . .

The day following Jesus would go forth into Galilee, and findeth Philip, and saith unto him, Follow me. John 1:43

. . . . . .

"I believe Mr. Maxwell was right when he said we must each one of us decide according to the judgment we feel for ourselves to be Christlike."

from *In His Steps*

. . . . . .

Jesus, help me keep my eyes on You. Remind me not to worry about what others are doing. Keep me focused.

I am come a light into the world, that whosoever believeth on me should not abide in darkness. John 12:46

• • • • • •

"Who were these people? They were immortal souls. What was Christianity? A calling of sinners, not the righteous, to repentance."

from *In His Steps*

• • • • • •

"We think we must climb to a certain height of goodness before we can reach God. But… if we are in a hole the Way begins in the hole. The moment we set our face in the same direction as His, we are walking with God."

—Helen Wodehouse

Thank You, Jesus, that no matter what happens in my life, I am eternally safe.

"There is no way that I know of," replied the pastor, "except as we study Jesus through the medium of the Holy Spirit. You remember what Christ said speaking to His disciples about the Holy Spirit: 'Howbeit when He, the spirit of truth, is come, He will guide you into all truth; for He shall not speak of Himself; but whatsoever He shall hear, that shall He speak; and He will show you things to come. He shall glorify me; for He shall receive of mine, and shall show it unto you. All things that the Father hath are mine; therefore said I, that He shall take of mine and shall show it unto you.' There is no other test that I know of."

from *In His Steps*

[Jesus] saith unto them, They that are whole have no need of the physician, but they that are sick: I came not to call the righteous, but sinners to repentance. Mark 2:17

• • • • • •

"It is easy to love an individual sinner, especially if he is personally picturesque or interesting. To love a multitude of sinners is distinctively a Christlike quality."

from *In His Steps*

• • • • • •

Fill me, Jesus, with Your love. Let me show that love to the world in concrete ways.

Be kindly affectioned one to another with brotherly love; in honour preferring one another; Not slothful in business; fervent in spirit; serving the Lord. Romans 12:10–11

• • • • • •

"I am absolutely convinced that Jesus in my place would be absolutely unselfish. He would love all these men in His employ. He would consider the main purpose of all the business to be a mutual helpfulness, and would conduct it all so that God's kingdom would be evidently the first object sought."

from *In His Steps*

• • • • • •

"Non-Christians and Christians both do social work, but non-Christians do it for something while we do it for Someone."

—Mother Teresa

23

I need Your wisdom, God.
My life seems so confusing.
Please show me what You
want me to do.

Now when Jesus heard these things, he said unto him, Yet lackest thou one thing: sell all that thou hast, and distribute unto the poor, and thou shalt have treasure in heaven: and come, follow me. And when he heard this, he was very sorrowful: for he was very rich. Luke 18:22–23

• • • • • •

Our Christianity loves its ease and comfort too well to take up anything so rough and heavy as a cross.

from *In His Steps*

• • • • • •

"We must offer the Lord whatever interior sacrifice we are able to give Him. . .even though our actions may in themselves be trivial."

—Teresa of Avila

For God giveth to a man that is good in his sight wisdom, and knowledge, and joy.
Ecclesiastes 2:26

• • • • • •

As he viewed his ministry now, he did not dare preach without praying long for wisdom. He no longer thought of his dramatic delivery and its effect on his audience. The great question with him now was, "What would Jesus do?"

from *In His Steps*

• • • • • •

"Pure wisdom always directs itself towards God; the purest wisdom is knowledge of God."
—Lew Wallace

What is that to thee? Follow thou me.
John 21:22

. . . . . .

How much had the members of the First Church ever suffered in an attempt to imitate Jesus? Was Christian discipleship a thing of conscience simply, of custom, or tradition? Was it necessary in order to follow Jesus' steps to go up Calvary as well as the Mount of Transfiguration?

from *In His Steps*

. . . . . .

Help me, Father, not to be a Christian simply out of habit or because it's socially acceptable. Show me how I need to change my life.

27

Shine Your light,
Christ Jesus,
on my path.

If any man serve me, let him follow me; and where I am, there shall also my servant be: if any man serve me, him will my Father honour.
John 12:26

. . . . . .

But the people had lately had their deepest convictions touched. They had been living so long on their surface feelings that when they had broken the surface, the people were convicted of the meaning of their discipleship.

from *In His Steps*

. . . . . .

"Make me firm and steadfast in good works, and make me persevere in thy service, so that I may always live to please thee, Lord Jesus Christ."

—Clare of Assisi

29

Whosoever he be of you that forsaketh not all that he hath, he cannot be my disciple.
Luke 14:33

• • • • • •

"I want to do something that will cost me something in the way of sacrifice. I am hungry to suffer something."

from *In His Steps*

• • • • • •

Show me how to give You everything, Jesus, the good parts and the bad, the big things and the small.

And he that taketh not his cross, and followeth after me, is not worthy of me.   Matthew 10:38

• • • • • •

"I have found my cross and it is a heavy one, but I shall never be satisfied until I take it up and carry it."

from *In His Steps*

• • • • • •

Give me Your strength, Lord, so that I can carry my cross.

Help me, Christ, to
walk in Your steps
even when it costs
me something.

Therefore if any man be in Christ, he is a new creature: old things are passed away; behold, all things are become new.

2 Corinthians 5:17

. . . . . .

The transformation of these…lives into praying, rapturous lovers of Christ, struck Rachel and Virginia every time with the feeling that people may have had when they saw Lazarus walk out of the tomb.

from *In His Steps*

. . . . . .

"God cannot reveal anything to us if we have not His spirit."

—Oswald Chambers

WHAT WOULD JESUS DO?

My sheep hear my voice, and I know them, and they follow me: And I give unto them eternal life; and they shall never perish, neither shall any man pluck them out of my hand.
John 10:27–28

. . . . . .

"Let us follow Jesus closer; let us walk in His steps where it will cost us something more than it is costing us now."

from *In His Steps*

. . . . . .

"When he asks for and receives our all, he gives in return that which is above price—his own presence. The price is not great when compared with what he gives in return; it is our blindness and unwillingness to yield that make it seem great."

—Rosalind Goforth

Righteousness shall go before him; and shall set us in the way of his steps.   Psalm 85:13

· · · · · ·

"What would Jesus do?" That question had become a part of his whole life now. It was greater than any other.

from *In His Steps*

· · · · · ·

Let my entire life, dear Christ, be focused on You. Be the center of my thoughts, the center of my work, the center of my love.

Take my fears, Jesus, take my worries. Take everything that holds me back from following You.

That ye might walk worthy of the Lord unto all pleasing, being fruitful in every good work, and increasing in the knowledge of God; Strengthened with all might, according to his glorious power, unto all patience and longsuffering with joyfulness.
Colossians 1:10–11

. . . . . .

"What is it to be a Christian? It is to imitate Jesus. It is to do as He would do. It is to walk in His steps."

from *In His Steps*

. . . . . .

"God can make you anything. . .but you have to put everything into His hands."

—Mahalia Jackson

37

Teach me, O Lord, the way of thy statutes; and I shall keep it unto the end. Psalm 119:33

* * * * * *

"Suppose that the church membership generally in this country made this pledge and lived up to it! What a revolution it would cause in Christendom!"

from *In His Steps*

* * * * * *

Start the revolution, my Lord, in my own life.

Seek ye first the kingdom of God, and his righteousness; and all these things shall be added unto you. Matthew 6:33

* * * * * *

"If I shall, in the course of my obedience to my promise, meet with loss or trouble in the world, I can depend upon the genuine, practical sympathy and fellowship of any other Christian who has, with me, made the pledge to do all things by the rule, 'What would Jesus do?'"

from *In His Steps*

* * * * * *

"You are not alone, you are in the Church. ... In that community you are sheltered and united with all those all over the world who believe in Christ."

—Hans Kung

Show me how to assess my
actions in Your light,
Jesus, rather than in the
dark of my own selfishness.